D0150767

TAJ MAHAL

© Rupa Classic India Series 1993
First published 1993 by Rupa & Co
7/16 Ansari Road, Daryaganj, New Delhi-110 002
Set in 9.6 on 12 Palatino by Printline, Daryaganj
Printed in India by Gopsons Papers Pvt. Ltd., Delhi
ISBN 81-7167-136-5

Design: Pankaj Goel
General Editor: Amrita Kumar

TAJ MAHAL

Rupa & Co

INTRODUCTION

The Taj Mahal is one of the world's acknowledged wonders. Its construction began in 1632 and was complete by the middle of the seventeenth century. Though the name of its architect remains a mystery, the inspiration was essentially that of the Mughal emperor Shah Jahan who employed 20,000 men to labour for twenty-two years to fulfil his dream of building for his queen, the finest mausoleum ever created by man.

The story behind the Taj Mahal is a poignant one. Mumtaz Mahal, Shah Jahan's queen and constant companion for nineteen years, even in battle, died giving birth to their fourteenth child in June 1631. It was said that for two years Shah Jahan lived the life of one in mourning. The story is also one of unbelievable opulence. Ancient records refer to the material used, to the white marble from Makrana and to the precious and semi-precious stones for the inlay work such as lapis lazuli and sapphires from Lanka, carnelian from Baghdad, turquoise from Tibet, agate from Yemen, coral from Arabia, garnets from Bundelkhand, diamonds from Jaisalmer, onyx and amethysts from Persia and so on. Tragically, most of this wealth was plundered through the years.

The Taj Mahal survived the outrage however, and people the world over continue to brave the relentless Indian sun, the narrow, dusty streets of Agra to visit a monument whose spirit no photograph can quite capture.

The main entrance to the tomb. The ornamentation of the Taj Mahal has a quiet elegance. Koranic inscriptions in the Arabic script and spandrels with inlaid arabesque do not detract from the beauty of the marble.

Mumtaz Mahal

Shah Jahan

Though the mimar-i-kul *or chief architect of the Taj Mahal remains unknown, the names of some of the artisans from Shah Jahan's ateliers were recorded. Among them were Chiranji Lal who patterned mosaics such as the one seen here, Ismail Afandi who built domes, Qazim Khan, a worker of precious metals, Amanat Khan Shirazi, a calligraphist and Amir Ali, a stone cutter.*

"The building I am speaking of is of a different and peculiar kind... It consists almost wholly of arches upon arches, and galleries upon galleries disposed and contrived in an hundred different ways."

Francois Bernier

Pages 12 and 13: *The filigreed marble screen set in frames* of pietra dura *encloses the cenotaphs of Mumtaz Mahal and Shah Jahan. It took ten years to make.*

Previous page: *Detail of inlay work on screen.*

The cenotaphs. In keeping with convention, the real graves lie in a dark crypt directly below (pages 20 and 21).

Overleaf: *Detail of inlay work on the cenotaphs.*

"Death: The essence of the Taj Mahal, yet more than death is here. Spirit rises from that central Islamic arch, a gothic pointer straining toward the white marble dome. It all becomes eerie and glorious, an invocation transforming death into some ultimate luxury."

Waldemar Hansen

The Taj Mahal took twenty-two years to construct during which 20,000 men worked incessantly. The river Yamuna was diverted in order to improve the view from the monument.

On either side of the Taj Mahal are two identical
buildings in red sandstone, with marble domes. On
the west of the mausoleum is a mosque; the one on the
east is called the jawab or answer.

Detail of arabesque inlay on the spandrels of the arches of the mosque and the jawab.

Right: *These three-domed structures provide architectural balance to the mausoleum and at the same time carry a magnificence of their own.*

The jawab is also known as the Mehman Khana as it is believed to have been used by travellers.

Within the mosque. Safeda *or white lead and* hirmichi *or red earth were used to decorate the ceilings in floral patterns.*

The rich, earthy red sandstone is offset by the white marble inlay framed in Koranic scriptures.

Right: *The boundary of the Taj Mahal overlooking the Yamuna.*

Overleaf: *The 30.5 m. high gateway of the Taj Mahal. Above the colossal archway rise eleven marble cupolas. At the corners of the structure are four towers topped by* chattris *or kiosks. It is through this lofty gateway that the visitor gets his first view of the mausoleum.*

"After examining the tout ensemble *from all possible positions, and in all possible lights, from that of the full moon at midnight in a cloudless sky, to that of the noon-day sun, the mind seemed to repose in the calm persuasion that there was an entire harmony of parts... on which it could dwell forever without fatigue."*
Colonel Sleeman

"*Did you ever build a castle in the air? Here is one, brought down to earth, and fixed for the wonder of ages.*"
Bayard Taylor

"... it seemed the embodiment of all things pure, all things holy and all things unhappy. That was the mystery of the building. It may be that the mists wrought the witchery..."

Rudyard Kipling

The garden is divided into four equal parts in the classic Persian *char* bagh *pattern. Apart from some rare trees, flowers such as narcissi, fritillaries, crocuses, irises and tulips could be seen here once.*

*The alcoves on the facade create a depth within the
vast expanses of marble.*

A glimpse of a minaret.

Calligraphy is an essential feature of Islamic architecture. Inscriptions served the dual purpose of displaying scriptural verse and ornamentation.

Overleaf: Pietra dura *was one of the glories of Mughal
architecture. Sometimes a single flower was composed of as
many as forty-eight pieces comprising stones such as lapis
lazuli, onyx, agate, jasper, topaz and carnelian.*

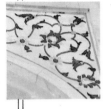

The arabesque motif is based fundamentally on geometric principles. Into these carved surfaces were embedded jewels from all over the world.

Right: *The dome is the crowning glory of the Taj Mahal. From the base to the apex of the finial it rises to a height of 44.40 m. Originally the finial was sheathed in 44,000 tolas of pure gold, plundered by British troops in 1803.*

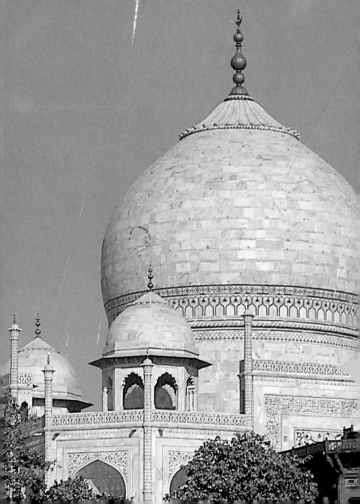

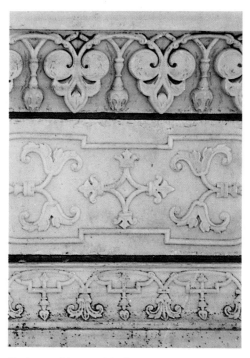

Detail of a marble panel in bas-relief.

Right: *The red sandstone plinth, paved with geometric mosaic. From its centre rises the 5.79 m. high marble plinth* (overleaf).

One of the four minarets that rise from the four corners of the plinth to a height of 40.23 m. Inside the minarets are winding staircases leading to the summit crowned with eight-windowed cupolas.

Right: *The mausoleum mirrored perfectly in the water channel that intersects the garden.*

Overleaf: *Detail of the dome.*

The pilasters are inlaid with yellow and black marble in horizontal chevrons.

Right: *The river Yamuna in spate. Three centuries ago Shah Jahan sailed through these waters in his royal barge.*

Overleaf: *View from the Agra fort where Shah Jahan was imprisoned by his son Aurangzeb and where he spent many solitary hours gazing at his beloved queen's mausoleum.*

"You knew, Shah Jahan, life and youth, wealth and glory, they all drift away in the current of time. You strove therefore, to perpetuate only the sorrow of your heart. Kingly power, stern as thunder, may sink into sleep like the glowing embers of the setting sun... Let the splendour of diamond, pearl and ruby vanish like the magic shimmer of the rainbow. Only let this one teardrop, this Taj Mahal, glisten spotlessly bright on the cheek of time, forever and ever."

Rabindranath Tagore

Photo Credits